Albert Eskeröd

SWEDISH FOLK ART

PHOTOS :   Nordiska Museet

DRAWINGS :   Maria Berkoff

CLICHÉS :   Grohmann & Eichelberg

PRINTED BY :   Boktryckeri AB Thule, Stockholm 1964

COPYRIGHT :   Nordiska Museet

NORDISKA MUSEET · STOCKHOLM

SWEDISH FOLK ART

A TRAVELLING EXHIBITION
IN THE UNITED STATES OF AMERICA
1964 — 1965

ORGANIZED BY
NORDISKA MUSEET, STOCKHOLM,
AND
SWEDISH INSTITUTE FOR CULTURAL
RELATIONS, STOCKHOLM.

CIRCULATED BY
THE SMITHSONIAN INSTITUTION,
WASHINGTON, D.C.

ACKNOWLEDGMENTS

Colorful ornament, innate purity of design, and respect for function have for generations characterized the work of the anonymous artisan in Sweden. Although parallels and influences can be traced in the folk art of this country, the quality and rich scope of Swedish folk culture is not widely known here. We are therefore especially honored to present this unique exhibition of masterpieces from three centuries of Swedish Folk Art.

The exhibition was made possible through the generosity of the Swedish Government, which cooperated with the Smithsonian Institution in every detail. We extend our warmest thanks to Dr. Gösta Berg, Director of the Nordiska Museet, and Dr. Per-Axel Hildeman, Director of the Swedish Institute for Cultural Relations, and members of their staffs for the time, thought, and energy they devoted to the show. The two institutions underwrote many of the costs in order to make the exhibition a reality.

We wish to acknowledge the invaluable assistance of Miss Eva Benedicks of the Swedish Institute, who served as a liason between the many individuals and organizations involved in the preparation of the show.

On this side of the Atlantic, we are deeply grateful to His Excellency Hubert de Besche, Ambassador of Sweden, who has consented to sponsor the six-museum tour in this country. Mr. Nils-Gustav Hildeman, Cultural Attache, and other members of the Embassy staff have also given us much assistance. We would like to thank Mr. Per Anger, Consul General in San Francisco, who has helped coordinate the opening of the exhibition during that city's Sweden Week.

The directors of the six participating museums have given their patient cooperation in attending to the details of presenting and circulating the exhibition. Furthermore, we appreciate the interest of Mrs. Helen Nelson Englund of the American-Scandinavian Foundation, who provided us with much useful information.

Finally, we wish to express our gratitude to the two organizers of the exhibition, whose spirit and guidance can be seen in every detail.

3

Mr. Tore Tallroth, in both his present position as Consul General in New York and his former work at the Swedish Institute for Cultural Relations, supervised the organization from start to finish. Dr. Albert Eskeröd, Chief Curator of the Nordiska Museet in Stockholm, selected the more than 500 objects to be included, and is thus responsible for the show's consistently high quality. Dr. Eskeröd's contributions include the writing of this catalogue and the accompanying captions, and the planning of the design and layout of the show.

ANNEMARIE H. POPE

Traveling Exhibition Service
Smithsonian Institution

CONTENTS

SWEDISH FOLK ART

THE COUNTRY AND ITS PEOPLE

Sweden has been called a country at the edge of eternal ice, and this was true about 14,000 years ago when the first primitive reindeer hunters migrated from southwestern Sweden to the edge of melting ice in the north. It was not until 9,000 years later, about 3,000 B.C., that agriculture was introduced into Sweden, probably as the result of a new wave of migration from the continent. The spread of a new culture throughout the country can be traced through the imposing tombs that the people built out of huge blocks of stone for their dead leaders. By the end of the Stone Age, the domesticated animals of later periods had already been introduced into the country.

Copper and bronze became known about 1,500 B.C., and the Bronze Age lasted for about 1,000 years. It was a period of outstanding skill in the use of metal for weapons and adornments. There were good trade contacts with continental Europe and the British Isles, from which the necessary metals were brought across the North Sea. The people of the Bronze Age knew how to build boats that were strong enough for open waters. Rock carvings of these boats as well as animals, scenes of agriculture, hunting and fighting, and symbolic signs have been found in the provinces of Bohuslän, Skåne and Östergötland. The people of this period buried their leaders under immense mounds of stone and earth. By the end of the Bronze Age, however, cremation became a more common practice, and from this, it may be assumed that a new conception of life after death had appeared.

About 500 B.C., when iron-smelting and the art of making iron tools was introduced into Scandinavia, a new natural resource was discovered — bog ore from the bottom of some of the lakes was used for making iron. This method was used in remote regions until the 19th century.

The first centuries after the birth of Christ of Scandinavian history are characterized by meager archeological finds, but there is evidence that the population decreased, and the climatic pattern apparently changed. There is a continuos discussion of how to interpret this. Most likely, the harshening climate and disease caused a decrease in the population. The change of climate made necessary the building of shelters for the cattle, which formerly grazed the pasturelands throughout the year. As the people slowly adapted themselves to the severe climate, they laid a foundation for a way of life that was to last for centuries. The people built to protect themselves, their cattle, and their crops. Gradually, this evolved into the country villages. By A.D. 400-500, the obligation of all free men to serve on the ships of the local kings had been introduced in Sweden. Throughout Europe, this period was characterized by population movements over vast regions, and this may have been caused by the climatic changes of the previous age. This period also witnessed German invasions that brought the Scandinavian people into close contact with distant parts of the European continent, particularly with the Mediterranean region.

The following centuries—the so-called Viking Age, A.D. 700-1,000 — were characterized by colonizing and lightning raids involving hundreds of ships from the Scandinavian countries. From the eastern and central parts of Sweden, Viking raiders invaded Russia and the Eastern Roman Empire; from the southern and western parts of Scandinavia, they turned towards western Europe and the British Isles.

The Viking Age was followed by a calmer period with friendlier contacts with western Europe. Missions from England and northern Germany gradually converted the heathen Vikings of the Scandinavian countries to Christianity. Churches were built, first of wood and later of stone; several hundred stone churches from the 12th and 13th century still remain in Sweden which, at that time, was a part of the huge Roman Catholic church. Cooperation between the leaders of the church and rival dynasties of kings resulted in a more organized society. Old provincial statutes were compiled into law books which regulated the life of the society from farming villages to the cities filled with trade and culture. Shortly after A.D. 1350, a national code was compiled. A separation of social groups occurred which made the clergy and the nobles tax-free landowners in the high service of crown and church.

By the end of the 14th century, Queen Margaret of Denmark effected a union of Denmark and Norway and, for a short period of time and with the help of Swedish nobles, also Sweden. Scandinavia was one kingdom. The system did not last very long, for Sweden was dependent on the Hanseatic League for a European market for metals, butter, and furs.

Christian II, king of Denmark, conquered Sweden in 1520. This was followed by a successful revolt against the Danes led by a young Swedish nobleman, Gustavus Eriksson Vasa, who, in 1523, at the age of 27, was elected king of Sweden. During his long reign (1523-1560), the national state of Sweden was founded. Vasa also introduced Lutheranism, which has remained the state church to this day. This justified to a certain degree Vasa's confiscation for the state of 21 percent of Swedish land, which had previously belonged to the Catholic church.

One hundred years later, the grandson of Gustavus Vasa, Gustavus II. Adolphus, fought as the leader of the Lutheran church in the Thirty Years War, a conflict that swept all of Europe. The peace treaty in 1648 gave Sweden opportunities for expansion, including a number of important possessions on the southern shore of the Baltic and on the North Sea.

These long wars made the kings dependent on the nobles, through the transfer or sale of crown lands and tax concessions in exchange for their services in the wars. The result was that the nobles, by the middle of the 17th century, possessed 72 percent of the land. At this point, the then King Charles XI, by a vote of Parliament, managed to reduce a large part of the estates. He reorganized the army and navy as standing forces. Soldiers lived on small farms, which had been put at their disposal by groups of farmers who equipped and armed them in lieu of paying taxes. This military organization, built up by Charles XI during two decades of peace and prosperity, enabled his seventeen-year-old son, Charles XII, to defeat Russia, Poland-Saxony, and Denmark. Despite these military successes, the long war was followed by a series of peace treaties after Charles XII's death in 1718, leaving the country with few of its earlier far flung possessions.

During the following 50 years, known as the "Era of Liberty," a real parliamentary system developed despite civil discord and political intrigue. It was during this era that Carl von Linné [Linnaeus] established his binomial system of scientific nomenclature, that Emanuel Swedenborg formulated his religious doctrines, and that the first soil reform was inaugurated. In 1771, Gustavus III ascended the throne; a year later, through a coup d'état, he gained even greater power. The last 20 years preceding 1809 are known as the "Gustavian Absolutism."

Many important cultural influences reached Sweden from France during this period. In 1809, after an unsuccessful war with Russia, Sweden ceded Finland to her. As a result, King Gustavus IV. Adolphus was dethroned, and his uncle became ruler as Charles XIII. A new constitution was drawn up to achieve a division of power between the ministry, representatives of the people, and the judiciary. Charles XIII was aged and childless when he ascended the throne in 1809, and as his successor one of Napoleon's famous marshals, Jean Bernadotte, was chosen. Bernadotte, as the heir apparent, handled Swedish policy from 1810 on and finally succeeded to the crown in 1818 as King Charles XIV. John. Sweden participated with her allies in the last coalition against Napoleon and, as a result, the Congress of Vienna in 1814 compensated Sweden by giving her Norway. This was a sort of compensation for her previous loss of Finland and possessions in northern Germany. Thus, Norway was forced into a union with Sweden; however, Norway's virtual independence and its new constitution were recognized, and finally, in 1905, the union was terminated peacefully.

From 1814 to the present, a period of 150 years, Sweden has enjoyed peace; this is one of the reasons for the country's present high economy and cultural growth. Growing class consciousness and expansion in agriculture, commerce, and industry, also led to a change in national representation in 1865; social changes had dispensed with the earlier differentiation of the four estates — nobles, clergy, burghers, and peasants — for this was no longer representative of the existing social structure of the country. The result was an introduction, and approval, in parliament of a body consisting of two elected chambers.

In the ensuing peaceful era, many important changes took place in Swedish society — so many that it is not possible to mention them in a short survey. However, the land reforms inaugurated by the Enclosure Act of 1827 were among the most important. This act resulted in the division of ancient village units, with their collective methods of working, into individually operating units, which in turn opened the way for more modern agricultural methods. Many Swedes regret the loss of the old integrated cultural life of the villages that was present before the reform; however, new land was settled and the population increased. This led to the great migration to the United States in the mid-19th century, culminating in the 1880's. The metal industry, with traditions dating from the 16th century, developed rapidly and served all branches of the economy. The vast forests became a rich resource, and steam-powered sawmills were erected along the shores as the demand for Swedish lumber from abroad grew. By the end of the 19th century, new technical processes had been developed that made the formerly worthless high-phosphorus iron ore of northern Sweden an important export item.

Industrialization and the great social changes in Sweden led to a changing of the old traditional world of the people, for more and more things that had previously been made in the homes were now manufactured in factories. A decline in tastes and skills was the unavoidable result. At the beginning of the 20th century, however, the handcraft movement began reviving the cultural heritage of folk art, using old forms as inspiration and models for modern work. This is one of the reasons for the high quality of contemporary Swedish handcraft and industrial design.

WHAT IS FOLK ART?

During the last half century different terms have been used to classify those groups of art that are not included in what art historians usually classify as the fine arts. Call it what you will — art populaire, folk art, peasant art, Volkskunst, Bauernkunst — this art of so-called "primitive people" is generally known as primitive art. Most of these terms are misnomers and should be abandoned because of their inadequacy and discrimination. In most parts of the world, we need no terms to define the social stratafications of art. On the other hand, in areas where society has been traditionally grouped for centuries into upper and lower classes, and where the leading class has been responsible for new trends in the history of art, the term "folk art" might well be applied. Such folk art frequently is characterized by its relation to the art of the leading group, which can be variously described as modern, upper-class, stylized, or fine art.

From this, we come to the characteristics of folk art. Perhaps folk art could be considered as the sum of those aesthetic and decorative values that belong, as a rule to every family within the local group. Also, this art is generally made within that group. It is an art applied to objects in daily use or for special use on festive occasions within either the family or the group as a whole. Folk art is old-fashioned and traditional in form and decoration; the same artistic elements and techniques have been employed for centuries, particularly in remote regions. When new influences arise, folk art blends the old forms and motifs with the new. Folk art has a rather strong social value within the group, and it frequently attains a special significance when supernatural beliefs and values are attached to special objects.

SWEDISH FOLK ART

In Sweden, few objects are left from the life of the common people that date to a period earlier than the middle of the 16th century. As a result, we cannot speak of folk art before that time. However, during the ensuing centuries, Sweden played an important role in the political life of Europe, and many Swedes came into closer contact with European culture than they ever had before. Officers who led Swedish armies on the European continent returned to Sweden and created homes in the image of what they had seen abroad. Men from foreign countries, skilled in the arts and sciences, settled in Sweden. All these influences drew the country more and more into the mainstream of European culture. In folk art, where medieval and pre-medieval cultures had been accepted for centuries, new elements were gradually assimilated. Dependence on old tradition during the assimilation process explains the differences between folk art and the more international fine art.

We can appreciate Swedish folk art during its time of greatness, from the mid-18th to the mid-19th centuries, because of the objects families still possess and from museum collections. After this century of greatness, industrialization spread over the country and cheap industrial products entered the homes. There was a withdrawal in the production and use of home-made things — a decline in folk art. The production of textiles, however, was preserved, particularly in the south-

*Chest from the early Middle Ages. Found in a store room of a farm
in Bjuråker, Hälsingland 1936. Now in the collection of Nordiska Museet.*

13

An interior from Dalarna with the fireplace and the "crown-rail".

ern part of the country; it was taken over, directly, by the handcraft movement, which got its start in Sweden just before the end of the last century. The renaissance in Swedish textiles had a beneficent effect on other small industries. There was an effort to bring new life into other folk arts, such as basketry, woodwork, straw fletching, iron-work, local dress (which now has an ever-growing popularity in Swe-den), and other things associated with the local traditions. The local associations for handcraft in the provinces have a central organization in Stockholm.

In general, Swedish folk art has the character of applied art in the sense that it is applied to objects of practical use — furniture for the home, tools used in either the fields or at home, household utensils, textiles for home use and for local dress. Though Swedish folk art, ge-nerally, has a practical usage, it also has a close connection with the pleasures of the people for their festivals and annual feastdays. The dress of the newborn child is as much a part of folk art as is the appar-

The living room in a farmhouse in Halland, decorated with textiles and painted wall hangings.

el of a bride and bridegroom. Many beautiful things have been carved and painted for the purpose of wooing a bride-to-be, and frequently these have been objects used for typically feminine farmwork — items used in flax-growing, weaving, washing, and ironing. For wedding gifts, there might be nicely painted furniture, textiles, or wall hangings for the home. At the annual festivals, especially Christmas, the finest objects in the peasant homes were used.

Much of Swedish folk art was produced regionally as a supplementary income by people with a lower standard of living than the average farmer. Thus, soldiers, cotters, craftsmen, and low-income farmers painted such things as wall hangings. The various poor regions of the country had their own specialities and from these developed leatherwork, ironwork, brass-casting, woodwork, cabinetmaking, straw-fletching, painting, weaving, and knitting. Aside from these, much Swedish folk art evolved from needs in the home or for use within the home. For example, the popular Dalarna horses were originally made by fathers as toys for their children while they worked in the forests and lived in special, collective huts. Along the coastal regions, young men,

15

A local artist in Dalarna, famous for his wooden horses and drinking bowls.

who were often sailors before they settled down at home, carved and decorated various objects for their sweethearts during their off-duty hours.

People once looked upon folk art as a type of collective art in which nearly every member of the community was a working craftsman. It has been said that folk art grew out of this collective effort; however, we know that this was not the case. Even if folk art, as well as the art of exotic peoples, is rather homogenous in various regions and the products are used daily by everyone, the craftsmen are, as a rule, individuals within their society. Even if they did not aim for individualism per se, their work often has special characteristics that permit attribution to particular artists, despite the fact that they lived 200 years ago and, as a rule, we do not know their names. It is also known that entire families could work in the same line of craft for a

16

couple of generations. Local artists have been, to a large degree, anonymous, but their work has had high artistic value.

It has often been said that folk art represents a degeneration from the art of the leading groups of society. This is true in the sense that the folk-art craftsman, living among the common people and working under poorer conditions than the leading contemporary artists, naturally had less skill and contacts in the more sophisticated fields of art. On the other hand, this lack of skill and sophistication gave his products a naiveté and a close connection with the traditional life of the common people. Also, it frequently resulted in an interesting variation between different cultural regions of the country. One must also remember that folk art is very conservative and maintains traditional patterns over the centuries, during which the old patterns blend very slowly with the new influences that filter down from the upper classes into the lower social strata. This trend is especially characteristic of the remote and isolated regions of the country where folk art, during the past centuries, has frequently preserved prehistoric and medieval patterns. Interestingly enough, folk art in regions where there was economic contact with the cities shows very dominating traits of the sophisticated art of the period. Thus, the function of Swedish folk art can be classified by both material and technique.

FOLK ART AND VILLAGE LIFE

From prehistoric times to the middle of the 19th century, Swedish

17

The farmers of a village in Västergötland, checking the height of the wooden fence.

people lived in villages where a collectivization and a close cooperation led to a good way of life. Each farmer had a seat in the village
guild, which was led by one farmer who acted as an elderman for a
year. This elderman was then succeeded by a neighbor at an "ordinary
meeting" which was generally held on the first day of May — the beginning of the agricultural year. The elderman called to the meeting
by blowing a horn, often nicely decorated, or notified the villagers
by having a messenger baton carried throughout the village. Frequently, each village had a stick with the marks or initials of each
farmer. The bookkeeping duties of each farm were controlled by
wooden sticks or rods (an abacus-type arangement) and, at the meet-
ings, the erring members paid their fines with beer, brandy, and meat
which were later used for a common feast. On such occasions, old-
fashioned drinking bowls were used and the ceremonies were remind-
ful of the old medieval guilds of the cities.

FOLK ART AND COLLECTIVE WORK

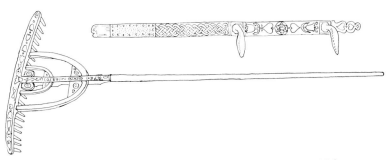

Before the breaking-down of the villages during the 19th century, there were many forms of collective work during which large groups of people came together. Also at the church, during market visits, festivals, and family celebrations people gathered together, and on these occasions a certain competition existed. There was a pride in the displaying of beautiful possessions. A young girl was proud of her nicely decorated rake for use during hay-making, a beautiful sickle for cutting corn was proudly shown, the scutching knife was displayed as well as the distaff and the mangling board. These items were wooing gifts from a young man as a sign of affection that also showed his skill

Haymaking in Skåne, when the nicely decorated rakes—often a wooing gift from the boy—were used.

in carving and painting. Furthermore, at the church, at the market place, and on other occasions when people from the farms, villages and parishes met, there was great pride in showing the best horses and the finest harnesses and bows, coverlets for the sleighs, cushions for the wagon seats, the most beautiful and expensive local costumes, and jewelry. During this period, before industrialization reduced the sense of beauty and quality of the country people and while many things within folk culture still resulted from personal skill and fancy, folk art played an important role in the social and cultural life of the country.

THE FARMER'S HOME

The traditional Swedish farms differed in various areas of the country. In the far north, log houses were constructed amidst coniferous forests; in the central Sweden, the country houses were built of partially timbered walls with vertical corner posts and horizontal boards lying between, as well as pure log houses; in the south, there were houses of mixed construction with half timbered walls and clay or brick between vertical posts and others of timbered walls between the supporting posts.

The square plan of the farmyards was the rule, although more open systems have been found in some regions. The farms had many individual buildings which were used for a variety of different purposes, a tradition dating back to the Viking and Medieval Ages, with a permanent tendency toward a closed farm. Upper-class influences, especially in the southeastern part of the country, have slowly led to more open systems with free-lying houses. After the Enclosure Act of 1827 and the breaking-down of the old villages, open plans were introduced throughout the country and many new farms were built.

Traditional Swedish farm houses have been, very often, a proof of

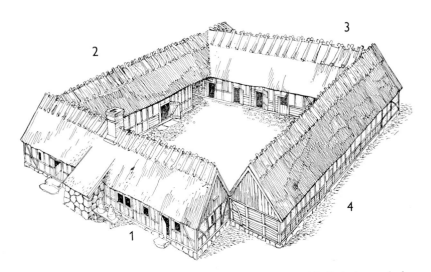

A typical squared farm from Skåne with walls of half timber and clay and with thached roof. Now at Skansen. 1 dwelling house, 2 and 4 barns, 3 stable.

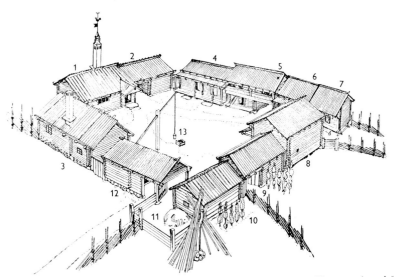

A typical farm with log houses from Dalarna. Now at Skansen. 1 and 3 dwelling-houses, 2 stable, 4-7 store-houses, 8-9 barns, 10 cowhouse, 12 store-house with a cellar.

good architectural taste and function. Influences from older architectural styles are often found in windows and entrances.

A variety of folk art can be found in the average farm home where the walls are decorated with textiles and painted wall hangings. A variety of furniture and house-hold implements can also be found.

TEXTILES

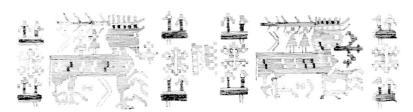

Textiles, a folk art by itself, have a rich heritage from past centuries in Sweden. Handmade textiles have become a dominant part of the handcraft movement, as well as factory-made textiles. The upsurge in the production of textiles has been most noticeable in Skåne, in southwest Sweden, in Dalarna, and portions of northern Sweden.

In Sweden, textiles have been used as woven or embroidered wall hangings; coverlets for beds, benches, sleighs and carriages; for tables and bed linens; and to embellish peasant dress. The ancient tradition of covering the walls of rooms with wall hangings began to die out in the 15th century, and was replaced by the painting of entire interiors. In the southwestern part of Sweden, however, the textile tradition is still alive today.

The art of weaving has shown different techniques. Some are very old and others, such as the so-called Flemish weaving, were taken over during the 18th century from the upper-class tradition. Even embroidery, to a certain degree, has preserved medieval aspects; different regions of the country have different specialities. Lace work, too, has shown local characteristics that have high artistic value.

Besides the technique, the patterns and motifs are of the greatest importance for the study of the history and diffusion of the textile

22

Deer and birds in low warp tapestry (rölakan). Skåne.

tradition within folk art. Many of the figural motifs have their origins in the fabled world of classical antiquity and the Middle Ages. Others go back to Biblical tradition, among them the A- and M-monograms that are found on the pendants of Scanian and Lappish jewelry. These symbols, such as the "Ave Maria," have been found woven into what is known as the "rölakan" technique, wich generation after generation of women weavers have reproduced without having any idea of its significance. Even newer motifs, such as parrots, swans, fruits and flowers, have found their way into folk art from the Flemish tapestry weaving.

23

*Adam and Eve in the Garden of Eden.
Embroided carriage cushion from Skåne.*

*Wall-hanging with the Three Magi.
Blekinge.*

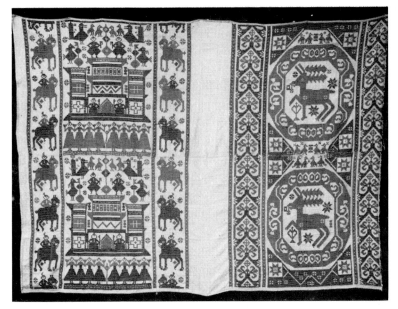

Wall-hanging from Skåne.

Bedcover, double-weaving. Bohuslän.

Bedcover, rug, in pile knot weaving, from northern Sweden.

WALL PAINTINGS

Wall paintings on cloth and later on paper are a folk art that is typically Swedish. This folk art flourished from the middle of the 18th century until the end of the 19th century. The motifs are generally Biblical, but there are also motifs from the daily life of the people or paintings of famous persons or events. In 1618, a new Bible was published in Sweden which had illustrations of 16th-century German woodcuts; these pictures were used as motifs by the provincial craftsmen in the north (covering the provinces of Dalarna and Hälsingland) and in the southern part of the country. It is interesting to note that many of the motifs, including the general technique of painting, had their origin in church painting of the Middle Ages and the Renaissance. The practical application, as shown in wall paintings, dates back to the old tradition of the use of textile wall hangings mentioned in the old Icelandic sagas. It is worth mentioning that peasant wall painting earlier has been known within larger regions of the country than those mentioned above. Also, there is from the well known later period a difference between the technique of wall painting of the northern and southern regions: in the south, the paintings were hung in the living room for decoration on festive occasions; in the northern regions, as a rule, the paintings were applied directly on the walls or ceilings, similar to murals, in rooms used for festive occasions. While using the motifs in the old tradition or as illustrated Biblical figures, the painters frequently dressed their figures — with the exception of Christ, His family, and His disciples — in the costumes of the period. In addition, colour was used in a free and individualistic manner.

27

*The Wise and the Foolish Virgins. The Three Magi.
Wall-painting from Småland.*

The Ascension of Elijah. Wall-painting from Dalarna.

Elias far till Simla med brinnande wagn och hästar Elisa detta ser och ropar Far min Far. 2.
Kon. B.2.C.

FURNITURE

Sweden is a forested country, and wood has always played an important role in the cultural inventory of the people. Walls and doors of houses are decorated with traditional ornaments. In the most remote parts of the country, so-called "crown-rails" have been used up to the present time. These have served a traditional legal function and are a decoration — complete with carved sides and dragonhead ends — that has survived from prehistoric times. These decorations were hung from the ceiling and divided the room into three parts, the least distinguished section being nearest the entrance and the most important section at the far end of the room, where the husband had his seat and where his weapons hung on the wall. The severest punishment was dealt any stranger who committed a crime in the section farthest from the entrance.

The furniture in the farmer's home often showed medieval, or even older, construction and decoration. The construction also showed a strong influence from the Renaissance period. When the painting of furniture became common during the mid-18th century, local artists showed great skill in decorative painting and frequently copied flowers and ornaments from the rococo wall paintings of the upper classes. Decoratively painted furniture are known particularly in Dalarna from the later 18th century where artists dealt with wall painting as well as painting of furniture. Their floral ornaments show a tendency toward an abstract type of decoration, particularly on cupboards and clocks.

Armchair from Skåne.

HOUSEHOLD IMPLEMENTS

Despite many available materials, wood was the most used material in the early days. Hollowed-out bowls were made from roots of trees, and natural forms of wood were used for decorative pieces. On household implements, the rule was that every piece, where practical usage made it possible, was decoratived. Geometric designs were the most common, but folk art also made use of such motifs as dragons, eagles, lions, horses, and birds –– many of prehistoric origin.

Sometimes, handles of objects or outstanding parts simulated human figures and animals. Free sculpture in folk art, though very uncommon in Sweden, took over from the tradition of fine art.

In Sweden, as in other Christian countries, one can find carved Christmas doves, a symbol of the Holy Ghost; pelicans feeding their young with blood from their breasts, a symbol of the Christian redemption. The tails and wings of the birds have been fashioned into fans with an excellent skill and with a knife as the only tool.

In olden times, the most used domestic utensils of the home were fashioned from wood. Despite the fact that few objects remain from a time preceding the 16th century, these few forms and decorations show a tradition that dates back to medieval and prehistoric times.

It is an old custom that the Swedish feast table not only provide a great abundance of food but also that the food be placed before guests in an attractive manner. Contributions of food by the guests were essential, since marriages and other important events in the family, as well as the annual festivals, were celebrated among the peasants

Chip-box for needle-work, Härjedalen.

and were a matter of concern for the whole village or, in some instances, for a whole region, which might have the same traditional celebrations. At weddings and christenings, each guest was expected to bring gifts such as bread, butter, cheese, porridge, and cakes. However, brandy and beer were generally contributed by the hosts. The containers in which these items were transported to the house where the feast would be held were executed with great care, and the peasants vied with each other in an attempt to display the finest baskets, butter-

A farmers family in the living room, Halland.

Richly decorated butter-mould from Härjedalen.

Mould for shaping the porridge, Blekinge.

boxes, or porrigers. Barley- and, later, riceporridge, which were principal dishes, were brought to the host's home in elegantly carved, wooden porridge kegs. Bread was brought in elaborately woven baskets, with painted decorations, made from roots or wooden chips. Each guest was expected to bring his own knife and spoon; the fork having only fairly recently been introduced into the peasant culture. The handle of the spoon was richly carved; frequently, it was a reminder of the days of courtship when such a utensil was given as a suitor's gift to his chosen one.

During these celebrations, wooden vessels of different types were used for the serving of food. Fish was served on wooden or earthenware dishes and these had small, hollowed-out cups in the center for a sauce into which the fish could be dipped. Meat was placed on another type of decorated wooden platter. Butter was made into decorative forms with the aid of a butter press or butter mold and was served on a "butter stool" or a "butter foot." Ale and brandy were as important to the feast as was the food, and ale was served from tankards or bowls

35

Bird-shaped drinking vessel from Härjedalen. Even used at weddings to collect gifts of money for the young couple.

of various types. The drinking vessels were of many types and varied from region to region: some were known as four-tipped, small bowls; bird shaped (ölgås or ale-goose), which floated in a big bowl; bowls with dragon-head handles of ancient type; goblets and beer-stoups were frequently decorated. For the serving of brandy, kegs and earthenware bottles, and later, glass bottles, were used. For the drinking of brandy in the peasant homes, a silver brandy cup was a prized possession.

Household utensils, even other than those used at the table (such as decorative cake stamps and cheese molds, canisters for flour and salt, and baskets of different types) were a matter for the local artists' skill. Bowls and baskets were quite necessary in the olden days, not only for household and personal things in the home, but also to serve as handbags and shopping bags for journeys. These were made in all sizes and

Drinking vessel showing how the local artist copied silver vessels in wood. Dalarna. Compare the silver vessel, page 55.

shapes, in both town and country, with simple or elaborate decorations.

Boxes for storing items of wearing apparel were larger and more ornate than those used for the storing of household items. These boxes for personal possessions were frequently decorated with the initials of the owner, an inscription, and a date. Many were betrothal gifts. When the box was presented to a girl, it might be filled with the beautiful things which her young man had made or bought for her.

The ancient "svep" technique was used in the making of many types of boxes. Long, thin fiber strips of wood were bent around a base and fastened to it. The ends overlapped and were stitched together with birch roots, generally in a decorative pattern. These boxes were oval or round and usually had ingenious snap-on lids. The woods used were generally birch, oak, beech, spruce or fir.

Chip-box from Jämtland.

Many wooden vessels were made of staves arranged around a solid wooden base which was held together by wooden hoops. Simple, hollowed-out vessels were made and used long before the staved vessels, but the staved type existed during the Viking era and probably long before that.

The decorations on wooden objects were accomplished in different ways. Early carvings were simple wood scratching. Another old type of decoration was an engraving, generally in a geometric pattern done with a knife, after which soot or lamp-black was rubbed into the incised design. Later, pointed and v-shaped instruments were used to produce relief carvings and a variety of repeated patterns. Carved ornaments are older than those that were burned or painted. By burning with metal stamps, iron pins, and wheels, craftsmen were able to make designs of broken lines or a monotonously repeated pattern of dots, circles, half-circles or s-forms — all of them traditional and many of prehistoric origin.

Wooden box with carved and painted decoration. Småland.

The oldest designs were usually geometric. Other styles echo the Renaissance period with animal figures in rows, and borders with interwoven, double-running, ribbon patterns, and symbolic signs and marks. There are, however, figural designs in Swedish folk art which originated in the medieval and prehistoric periods. The rococo influence swept through Sweden in the latter part of the 18th century. A naturalistic floral decoration was introduced into the old carvings and, slowly, this became a pattern in folk art. Local artists have produced things of high quality in such items as painted furniture and household objects.

BASKETRY

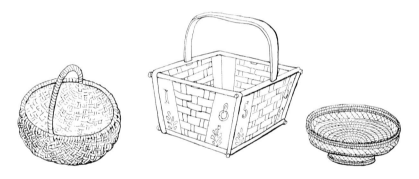

Basket weaving has played a large role in the field of Swedish folk art. For many years, it was a craft pursued by the poor, the disabled, and the aged. Most of the baskets were made for practical use, but some were used for festival occasions and these were woven in decorative, open-work patterns. Simple baskets were made to hold such things as fish, salt, roots, and vegetables. Larger straw baskets were used for grain and flour. Baskets were woven or coiled from various lengths of twigs, roots, wooden strips, bast fiber, or straw. There are many local traditions within this field of folk art. Today, together with the textile art, basketry is very much favored by the modern Swedish handcraft movement.

40

A basket-maker at work. Värmland.

A material used for the ancient "svep" technique as well as for weaving has been birch bark. Small boxes of different types and sizes are made of this bark. The technique itself is a decorative element, and the surface of the smooth material, soft as leather, is covered with an attractive geometrical design. The use of birch bark is most noticeable in those regions of Sweden that were colonized by the Finns as early as the 16th century.

41

Baskets woven of birch roots.

Snuff boxes of birch-bark with geometrical ornaments. The dark parts of the smaller one are painted in green.

CERAMICS

While wooden objects have been used by the Swedish peasant from olden days to the middle of the 19th century, ceramic pieces for storing foods and for festive serving dishes are only known to have been used since the mid-17th century. The use of wooden rather than ceramic objects resulted from the fact that wooden pieces could be made at the farm, while ceramics were made by local potters or in small local factories, or in the cities, and the articles had to be purchased. However, when ceramic pieces, as well as pewter and silver objects, were acquired for the home, they were a sign of wealth and became the pride of the peasant woman. She usually had such possessions neatly arranged on the inner gabled wall of the living room where the head of the house sat.

The oldest ceramic pieces are brown in color with yellow and green ornamentation. Later, the base color was usually pale yellow with the decorations in green, red-brown, lilac-black, and sometimes, white. The ornamentation on the ceramic pieces does not differ greatly in the various regions of the country and is usually dotted or curved lines, stylized tulips, roses, birds, and other conventional figural motifs. Swedish ceramic art shows an intimate connection with that on the European continent. It reveals an art tradition that spread during the past few centuries through people who have dealt with handcraft as both a rural and an urban profession.

Puzzel-jug from Småland.

Ceramic dipper for candle making. Blekinge.

I RONWORK

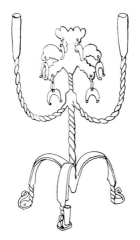

Swedish ironwork shows an unbroken technical tradition dating back to prehistoric times. Province laws of medieval times refer to the smiths as a special class of rural craftsmen. The village smith made all sorts of objects for everyday use. Sometimes a particular item was sold in the surrounding districts, and from this grew regional specializations. During the second half of the 17th century, it became easier in Sweden to obtain good iron. Iron handcraft was in vogue, and the rural smiths became prosperous and artistically ambitious. Until the middle of the 19th century, they created objects of great artistic value. At this time, the use of cast iron from new factories spread over the country, thus sounding the death knell to the work of the artistic blacksmith.

There have been four distinct fields where rural ironwork has produced objects of artistic value: objects for the fireplace; candlesticks; grave crosses; and mounts for windows and doors.

Through the Swedish handcraft associations, an attempt was made at the end of the 19th century to revive the craft of artistically wrought ironwork, and the effort was successful. Objects for the fireplace and candlesticks that are artistically beautiful are now available, and ironwork is a growing branch within the modern handcraft movement.

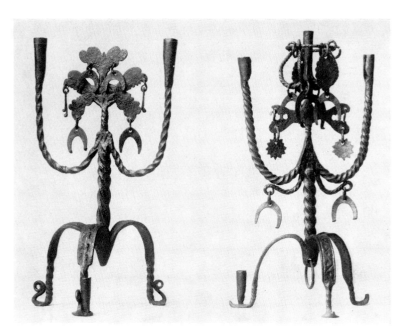

Candlesticks from Skåne.

While the candlesticks above give evidence of traditions from the Middle Ages and a development typical for southern Sweden, the grave crosses appeared during the 18th century and was a speciality for western Sweden. In both cases they are wrought by the village blacksmith. Characteristic for Swedish wrought iron of this kind are the small decorative hangings, which in Skåne were shaped like horseshoes while they in the rest of Sweden were shaped like the leaves to be seen on the grave cross to the right. These leaves are known since pre-historic times.

Grave-cross of iron from Värmland.

48

LOCAL COSTUMES, DRESS ORNAMENTS, AND JEWELRY

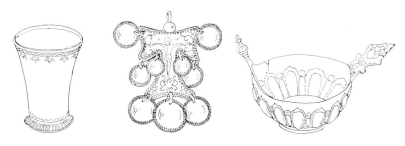

The first acquisitions of Arthur Hazelius in 1872 for his newly created Nordiska Museet were some peasant costumes from the province of Dalarna. Since then, increasing this collection has been one of the museum's most important activities.

As with so much folk culture, peasant costumes show influences from many previous periods, and these influences differ in the various regions according to the economic conditions, the amount of contact with the upper class, and urban fashions. In remote regions of the country, more of the medieval or even prehistoric elements have been preserved. In areas near the large cities or surrounding the manorial estates in the country, peasant costumes are similar to urban and upper-class fashions. Thus, one single costume may combine elements from several different periods, and most of these seem to have been adopted more or less by chance. As a result, each local costume has its own history.

Even within the same parish different costumes were used, though on different occasions. In the parish of Vingåker, for example, the everyday garments were largely influenced by late 18th- or early 19th-century fashions; however, festival dresses show definite medieval and 17th-century traits. As a rule, the peasant woman had one everyday dress, one dress for Sundays and holidays, and one for occasions such as festivals, weddings, and funerals. And places exist where the peasant costumes have played such a prominent role in the local society that rules were made to correlate the dress with the church year.

There was an important and a respected difference between the dress

Christmas morning in Mora, Dalarna, showing the rich use of fur-jackets in winter time. Painting by Anders Zorn.

A peasant couple from southern Skåne.

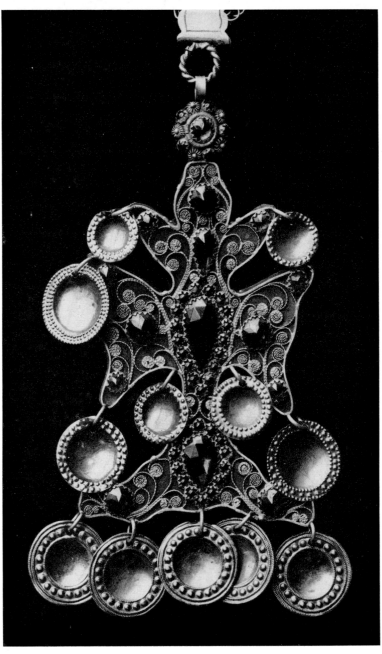

Bridal ornament from Skåne.

of a married and a single woman. One common rule was that the woman covered her hair after marriage.

Different clothes were worn during summer and winter, and the changeover was made on a certain day of the year. In northern Sweden, leather was frequently used for the winter dress.

During the past century peasant costumes have become very popular. Interest in them has spread more and more from their origin with the country people to urban groups. Special organizations arrange dances where the old, local costumes are worn, and this gives a common acceptance to this folk art.

Peasant dress ornaments are generally included in what we consider folk art, even though they were fabricated by silversmiths in the cities. These silversmiths followed the demands and tastes of the peasants, and in the case of dress and ornaments, the rural population was very traditional minded. Dress ornaments were born by the bride and the married woman, who had no trouble in deciding which pieces to wear — she simply wore all she had. From a modern point of view, a rich country woman could look rather overloaded. The married woman's rings, necklaces, hangings, buttons, buckles, clasps, belts, pins, and lacing stays were originally functional details of her dress, but over the centuries these things became more and more decorative. And the fact should not be overlooked that these decorations also had social significance in that they showed the wealth of the family.

The pendant worn around the neck is an ancient type of ornament; with the introduction of Christianity into Sweden, the prehistoric "brakteater" acquired a new symbolism. Round and T-formed pendants were embellished with IHS monograms, crucifixes, and the monogram A and M (for Ave Maria) of medieval design. Pendants of a special type are the "ellakors" (elves' crosses), which had to be fabricated in magical ways as, for example, from nine different pieces of inherited silver. These crosses had to be collected and paid for in silence at the silversmith's shop. If everything was accomplished in the proper manner, the "ellakors" were a neverfailing, supernatural protection against sickness and all kinds of evil powers.

Peasant art in this field includes other kinds of ornaments for the traditional dress, such as rings, clasps, rings for lacing stays, cloak buck-

Silver vessel. Compare the wooden vessel, page 37.

les, decorative buttons, and many others too numerous to describe. Two objects, however, that deserve special mention are the bridal belt and the bridal crown. The use of a belt with the female dress has been used since prehistoric times, and the bridal belt is a part of this tradition. It was one of the gifts that the bridegroom was expected to give his bride. The bridal crown, in the Christian tradition the attribute of the Virgin Mary, has become a symbol of virginity, and the bride was allowed to wear the crown only if she deserved to do so. The bridal crown and the religios ceremony performed by the cleric was slowly accepted into the folklore tradition, replacing the older ceremonial exchange of gifts by which the wedding was considered to be legalized. By a synod decision in 1584, it was determined that the churches should melt down their unused pieces of silver and make this silver into crowns that could be lent to brides for their wedding ceremonies. Because they were church property, these bridal crowns were valuable pieces. Through the years, the design of these crowns has changed from the early large, heavy crowns to the smaller ones of this century.

Obviously, ordinary peasants in earlier times could not possibly manage to own valuable pieces of gold and silver. However, it has been an old and common custom among country people to buy silver objects, particularly spoons and drinking cups, as a type of saving to be used only for real need. These pieces, as a rule, were engraved with the initials of the farmer who acquired them.

ANNUAL FESTIVALS

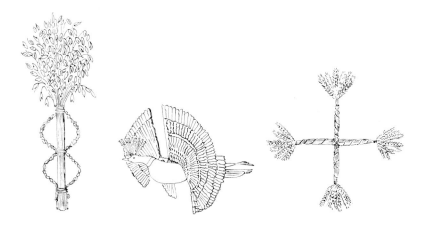

Although real folk art is generally applied to tools and implements for everyday use, it has a special relationship to the feasts of the church as well as festivals of the people.

The agricultural year provides a natural rhythm of periods of hard labor and periods of quiet and rest. Correlated with this natural system are the traditional festivals of the church, which had their origins in a foreign culture. The result has been a mixed and, frequently, contradictory pattern in the social life in which folk art plays a rather important role.

The multicolored Shrovetide scourges with their origin in Christ's

Tilting the ring, a competition by the young men of the village on Shrove Monday in Skåne.

scourge, nowadays fill the market places and decorate the homes, making a new tradition of an old Christian custom. The cock, the Christian symbol of resurrection, has grown from an unimportant position in folk art into a very popular product of modern handcraft, especially used at Eastertide. The may-poles used in the celebration of midsummer in local communities were once very genuine products of folk art, but are used less frequently today.

Festivals at the end of the harvest have not been as popular in Sweden as on the continent. However, in the southern part of Sweden, a harvest doll was made at the end of the harvest; in Värmland, when the last of the oats was harvested, straws were plaited and hung in the living room. It was a custom on Christmas morning to give these harvest knots to the cattle.

According to an old Swedish legend, the night of December 13, Lucia Night, was said to be the longest night of the year, and it was therefore necessary to give a very early morning meal to the people

57

A modernization of the Christmas dove with a splendid tail, by the local artist called "the peacock". Sörmland.

of the house and the cattle. This early meal provides the background for the present Lucia tradition, when a young girl with a tiara of burning candles on her head serves coffee and a special "Lucia bread" in the early morning hours. This quaint custom has spread from Sweden to many other parts of the world, including the United States.

During the Christmas season, the farmer's home was traditionally decorated with his most valuable possessions. Wall paintings and textiles covered the walls. The finest things were used on the table for

Cake baked at Christmas and used as a food of special strength at plowing and sowing in spring.

the special festive meal served on Christmas eve. Wooden doves, the symbol of the Holy Ghost, or crowns of straw, were suspended over the table. Crosses made of straw or rush protected the family against evil things at Christmas. A Yule goat made of straw was used in children's games or for decoration. When baking bread for Christmas, a special "sowing-cake" was frequently made. It was kept on the table during the Christmas season and then was used as a kind of good-luck food for the draft animals or put into the sowing-basket in the spring. Going to church in heavy snow on Christmas morning, the farmer proudly showed his decorated sleigh and harness for the horses. Christmas was not only a time for preserving traditional customs and religious feeling, it was also time of rest, and the farm home was made as pleasant and beautiful as possible.

FROM THE CRADLE TO THE GRAVE

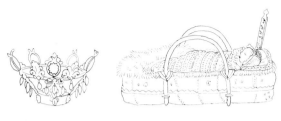

The newborn child in the old farming village entered a world of friendliness and beauty. Neighborhood wives brought appetizing food to the mother in nicely decorated chipboxes and baskets. The robe and cap used at the christening, like the cradle at home, frequently were products or real folk art. In Dalarna, it was customary to use a special christening bag in which was placed a small, carefully carved stick with the name and birthdate of the child.

On her betrothal, a girl received a bridal box containing gloves, a

Christening bag with christening stick. Dalarna.

Bridal crown of gilded brass. Uppland.

ring, often a silk scarf, and sometimes a necklace. The bridegroom might be given embroidered gloves, braces, or a shirt. Wedding greetings and paintings were produced by local artists, who also made birthday cards, name-day greetings, and memorial pictures in memory of a deceased member of a family. Frequently, these memorial pictures were hung in the church.

"The Ages of Man" or "From the Cradle to the Grave" are rather popular motifs for wall paintings and for decorative linings for the insides of chests. Within the old farming society, the ages of man were well integrated, and the ceremonial seasons of human life played an important role, which is evident in the varying forms that folk art has taken.

MODERN SWEDEN AND THE OLD FOLK ART

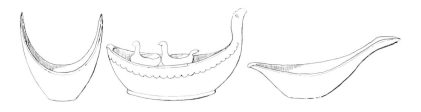

Much more could be written about Swedish folk art, its history, its forms, and its function, than is possible in this short survey.

The quality of the articles produced both in the farm homes and by the local artists and craftsmen proves that folk art was a living reality up to the end of the 19th century. The rise of industrialism threatened to end handcraft in Sweden and elsewhere; nearly everything could be turned out by the factories, and buying ready-made things in the village store was easier than laboriously making them by hand. New materials and new aniline dyes resulted in a decline in those things which were formerly made in the homes. As the old traditions and handcrafts disappeared, nothing worthwhile appeared to take their place.

At this critical period in the 1870's, Artur Hazelius foresightedly started on his life work of creating the Nordiska Museet. In this museum and in other more recently established local museums, very large and representative collections of Swedish folk art and handcrafts have been preserved. These collections of folk art have from the beginning played an important role in the rebirth and renewal of folk art through the modern handcraft movement. Originally, this interest was largely confined to the upper classes; however, it was steadily broadened to new groups, and organizations were formed to take care of the new program. At the Stockholm exhibition of 1897, by which time half of the Nordiska Museet had been built, a large collection of old and contemporary folk art and handcraft was on display. For Lilli Zickerman, the pioneer of modern Swedish handcrafts, this exhibition marked a turning point. As one of those arranging the displays, she said afterwards, "My eyes were opened, and I saw for the first time how beauti-

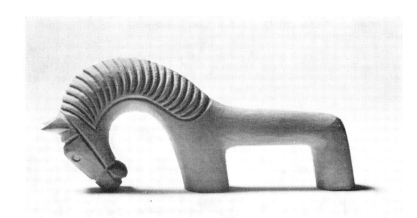

Nowadays, the horse from the mangling board is used as a decoration only.

ful and right the old handcrafts were, and how degenerate and ugly the new things appeared in comparison. After that, I could never let go the conviction that the old must be saved, and the new guided along the proper courses before it was too late."

The first Swedish handcraft society (Föreningen Svensk Hemslöjd) was organized in 1899 by Lilli Zickerman. Since then, many local hand-

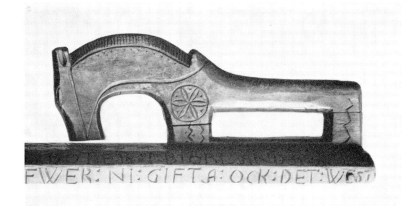

The traditional form for handle to a mangling board.

A contemporary bird-shaped drinking cup. The concentric layers in the wood are consciously used as decoration.

craft organizations have been started in Sweden, and they play an important role in Swedish cultural life. In 1912, these various organizations were consolidated into Svenska Hemslöjdsföreningarnas Riksförbund, which placed a special emphasis on the sale of handcraft.

Swedish handcraft is considered to be rather advanced in technique and taste. However, its feeling for quality, its simplicity and functional form, and its local flavor have their roots in traditional folk art. Contemporary designers and artists are currently using Swedish folk art as an important source of inspiration.

THE LAPPS AND THEIR FOLK ART

Of the 35,000 Lapps who live in the northern parts of Sweden, Norway, Finland, and the Soviet Union, about 10,000 live in Sweden. A commonly held belief is that all the Lapps are nomads who tend their reindeer flocks; however, about two-thirds of the Lapps in Sweden occupy themselves as fishermen, farmers, and forest workers. The general social and economic interests of all the Swedish Lapps are represented by a union of their own, Svenska Samernas Riksförbund.

The Lapps are the only European polar people; they have lived in rather close contact with Nordic people since prehistoric times. Their contact with the Swedes dates from the 14th century. This cultural contact over the centuries has resulted in many similarities between Lappish and Swedish folk art. Nevertheless, the folk art of the Lapps has its own character, due to its special environment and traditions.

Since the early 16th century, the nomads who tend and breed reindeers have had a dominating position in comparison with other groups. From a rather casual type of living — their own individual fishing, hunting, and the tending of small flocks of reindeer — they have built up a very specialized kind of reindeer-breeding. This is particularly true among the mountain Lapps. Their exceptionally nomadic way of life has resulted in small, light-weight art objects.

The relative isolation that has characterized the European polar area to the present has fortunately preserved the ornamental traits of Nordic folk art that date back to Viking and medieval times. In addition, the Swedes have looked upon the Lapps as being particularly clever in black magic, probably because the Lapps were not Christianized until the 17th and 18th centuries.

Because of current monetary incentive, the Lapps are nowadays more interested in handcrafts than before. And handcrafts, as well as the language, are considered to be the cultural elements that have the

65

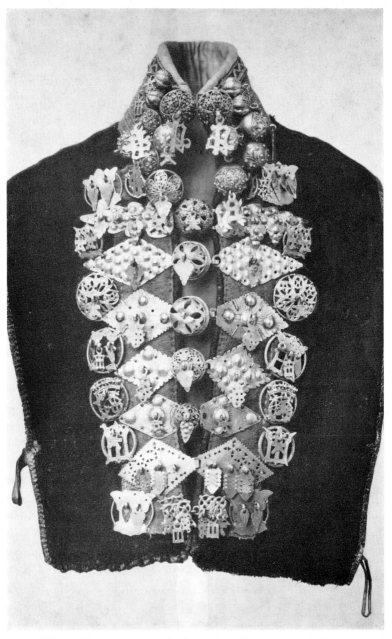

Silver collar for a woman's dress. Note the many pendants of A- and M-monogram (Ave Maria—). Central Lappland.

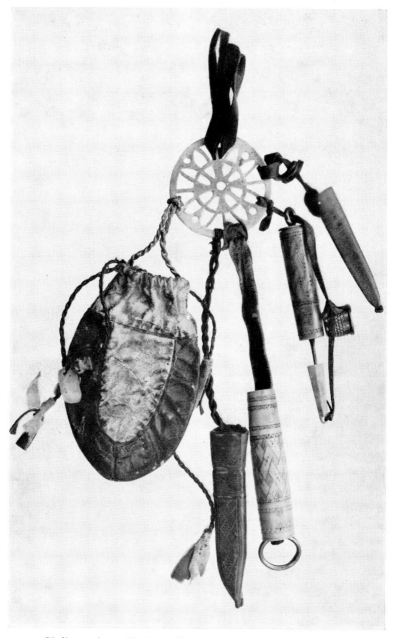

Girdle pendants. Tools of different use for the woman's dress. Central Lappland.

A group of present day Lappish handcraft. Tin embroideries and a bridal crown made of birch roots. Photo. Pål Nils Nilsson, Stockholm.

best chances of survival. Fortunately, an everincreasing professional handcraft is emerging today, making use of the old traditional materials, techniques, decorations, and forms in beautiful ways and often for new purposes. A central organization in Sweden, Same Ätnam, is working for the preservation and revival of Lappish handcraft.

The Lapps of today are generally called *Sames*, a name derived from their own language.